With Love to a Wonderful Mother

With Love To A Wonderful Mother

Beautiful Writings in Tribute to Mothers

Selected by Kitty McDonald Clevenger

Hallmark Editions

The publisher wishes to thank those who have given their kind permission to reprint material included in this book. Every effort has been made to give proper acknowledgments. Any omissions or errors are deeply regretted, and the publisher, upon notification, will be pleased to make necessary corrections in subsequent editions.

Acknowledgments:
"Everyday Madonna" by Richard Armour. Reprinted by permission of the author. "I'd Rather" from *Poems to Mother* by Meredith Gray. Copyright 1937 by Crescendo Publishing Company. Reprinted by permission of Robert L. Bell, Melrose, Mass. 02176. "A Mother's Prayer" from *Shining Rain* by Helen Welshimer. Copyright 1943 by Helen Welshimer. Renewal copyright © 1971 by Ralph Welshimer. Reprinted by permission of the publishers, E. P. Dutton & Co., Inc. Proverbs 31:25-28 from the *Revised Standard Version of the Bible*. Copyrighted 1946, 1952, © 1971, 1973. Reprinted by permission of the National Council of the Churches of Christ. "The Perfect Mother" from *The Exile* by Pearl Buck. Copyright 1936 by Pearl S. Buck. Copyright Renewed. Reprinted by permission of Harold Ober Associates Incorporated. "When Mother Sleeps" from *Just Folks* by Edgar A. Guest. Copyright 1917 by Reilly & Lee Company, a division of Contemporary Books, Inc. Reprinted by permission. "The Way of a Mother" by Katherine Edelman. © 1954 by Katherine Edelman. Reprinted by permission. "Half-Past Three" from *The Gypsy Heart* by Emily Carey Alleman. Copyright 1957 by Emily Carey Alleman. Reprinted by permission.

Photographs:
Richard Fanolio, pages 32, 46; Farrell Grehan (Photo Researchers), page 29; Carol Hale, pages 5, 40; Maxine Jacobs, title page, pages 13, 24, 37; Fred Kautt, page 21; Nancy Matthews, page 16; Sue Morey, dust jacket cover, page 8.

The Perfect Mother

...Never was a woman more richly mother than this woman, bubbling over with a hundred little songs and scraps of gay nonsense to beguile a child from tears, and filled with wayward moods as she was; yet her hands were swift to tenderness and care and quiet brooding tending when need arose. Never was she more perfect mother than during the summers on the mountaintop when she could give herself freely to her children. She led them here and there in search of beauty, and she taught them to love cliffs and rugged rocks outlined against the sky, and to love also little dells where ferns and moss grow about a pool. Beauty she brought into her house, too, and filled the rooms with ferns and flowers.

Pearl S. Buck

The real religion of the world comes from women
much more than from men —
from mothers most of all,
who carry the key of our souls in their bosoms.

Oliver Wendell Holmes

The many make the household,
But only one the home.

James Russell Lowell

My Mother

Who fed me from her gentle breast,
And hushed me in her arms to rest,
And on my cheek sweet kisses pressed?
          My Mother.

When sleep forsook my open eye,
Who was it sang sweet lullaby,
And rocked me that I should not cry?
          My Mother.

Who sat and watched my infant head,
When sleeping on my cradle bed,
And tears of sweet affection shed?
          My Mother.

When pain and sickness made me cry,
Who gazed upon my heavy eye,
And wept for fear that I should die?
          My Mother.

Who dressed my doll in clothes so gay,
And taught me pretty how to play,
And minded all I had to say?
          My Mother.

Who ran to help me when I fell,
And would some pretty story tell,
Or kiss the place to make it well?
          My Mother.

Who taught my infant lips to pray,
And love God's holy book and day,
And walk in wisdom's pleasant way?
          My Mother.

And can I ever cease to be,
Affectionate and kind to thee,
Who was so very kind to me?
                My Mother.

Ah! no, the thought I cannot bear,
And if God please my life to spare,
I hope I shall reward thy care,
                My Mother.

When thou art feeble, old and gray,
My healthy arms shall be thy stay,
And I will soothe thy pains away,
                My Mother.

And when I see thee hang thy head,
'Twill be my turn to watch thy bed,
And tears of sweet affection shed,
                My Mother.

For God, who lives above the skies,
Would look with vengeance in His eyes,
If I should ever dare despise
                My Mother.

                                Jane Taylor

Only a Mother

There are times when only a mother's heart
Can share the joy we feel
When something that we've dreamed about
Quite suddenly is real!
There are times when only a mother's love
Can understand our tears,
Our bitter disappointments
And all our childish fears.
There are times when only a mother's words
Can make us want to smile
And give us the assurance
That makes life more worthwhile.
There are times when only a mother's faith
Can help us on life's way
And inspire in us the confidence
We need from day to day.
Yes, so often through our lifetime,
Whether skies are gray or blue,
It seems that there are countless times
When only a mother will do.

Mary Dawson Hughes

No joy in nature is so sublimely affecting as the joy
of a mother at the good fortune of her child.

Jean Paul Friedrich Richter

Mother in gladness, Mother in sorrow,
Mother today, and Mother tomorrow,
With arms ever open to enfold and caress you,
O Mother of Mine, may God keep you and bless you.

An Old English Prayer

Mother's Recipes

Most women have a pantry filled
With spices, herbs and stuff,
Salt and sugar, yeast and flour,
But that's not quite enough.
My Mom's the finest cook on earth,
And she told me long ago
That bread's no good unless you add
Some loving to the dough.
"And when you're baking pies," says she,
"A pinch of faith and trust,
If added to the shortening, makes
A tender, flaky crust;
And compassion by the spoonful
In the batter of a cake
Makes it come out light and fluffy,
Just the finest you can make."
Now these things can't be purchased
In the store across the way,
But Mother keeps them in her heart
And uses them each day.

Reginald Holmes

As soft and gentle
        as candlelight —
Ever welcoming,
        ever bright —
          this is a mother's love.

Amy Cassidy

Where we love is home.
    Home is where our feet may leave
        but not our hearts.

Oliver Wendell Holmes

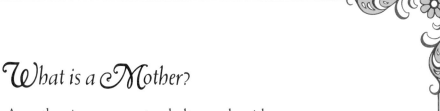

What is a Mother?

A mother is someone to shelter and guide us,
To love us, whatever we do,
With a warm understanding and infinite patience
And wonderful gentleness, too.
How often a mother means swift reassurance
In soothing our small, childish fears,
How tenderly mothers watch over their children
And treasure them all through the years!
The heart of a mother is full of forgiveness
For any mistake, big or small,
And generous always in helping her family,
Whose needs she has placed above all.
A mother can utter a word of compassion
And make all our cares fall away,
She can brighten a home with the sound of her laughter
And make life delightful and gay.
A mother possesses incredible wisdom
And wonderful insight and skill —
In each human heart is that one special corner
Which only a mother can fill!

Katherine Nelson Davis

One of a Kind

Her warm words of praise,
    a kiss on the cheek,
The language of love
    that she knows how to speak —
These are the reasons
    a mother's unique.

Susan Bennett

Mother Love

What is mother love?
    the flame
    that kindles tribute
        to her name...
    that lights our path
        and guides our aim...
    this is mother love.
What is mother love?
    the flower
    whose fragrance sweetens
        every hour...
    that never fades through
        sun or shower...
    this is mother love.
What is mother love?
    the smile
    that lifts our thoughts
        to things worthwhile...
    that warms and brightens
        every mile...
    that is mother love.

Margaret Benton

This is a Mother

Mother — no word on earth can evoke more beautiful
thoughts or more affectionate feelings. She is our
first experience of tenderness, our earliest wisdom.
Hers are the patience and kindness we grow on, the faith
and inspiration we live by — the warmth and devotion
we treasure through the years. Put them all together
and they spell love.

Edward Cunningham

Dear Mother

Dear Mother, when I think of you
　　I think of all things good and true,
Of trees and lanes and babbling brooks,
　　Of mountains, hills and shady nooks.

I think of flowers of every hue,
　　Of roses kissed by morning dew,
Of violets blue and daisies bright,
　　And stately lilies, pure and white.

I think of cloudless skies of blue,
　　And, Mother dear, because of you,
I think of robins in the spring
　　And of the joyous songs they sing.

I think of fields of golden grain,
　　And of the soft refreshing rain.
I think of honeybees in clover
　　And of God's sunshine bubbling over.

I think of children's happy faces,
　　Of grand old ladies in their laces,
Of all men, noble, brave and true,
　　Because of Mothers just like you.

Pauline Mengedoth

She was always there
　　　　and would always wear
a smiling face;
　　　　she gave advice,
　　　　　　a helping hand,
a warm embrace —
　　　　my mother.

Kay Andrew

Story of My Life

I cannot recall what happened during the first months
after my illness. I only know that I sat in my mother's
lap or clung to her dress as she went about her household
duties. My hands felt every object and observed every
motion, and in this way I learned to know many things.
Soon I felt the need of some communication with others
and began to make crude signs. A shake of the head
meant "No" and a nod, "Yes," a pull meant "Come" and a
push, "Go." Was it bread that I wanted? Then I would
imitate the acts of cutting the slices and buttering them.
If I wanted my mother to make ice cream for dinner I
made the sign for working the freezer and shivered,
indicating cold. My mother, moreover, succeeded in
making me understand a good deal. I always knew when
she wished me to bring her something, and I would run
upstairs or anywhere else she indicated. Indeed, I owe
to her loving wisdom all that was bright and good in my
long night.

Helen Keller

A Mother's Picture

A lady, the loveliest ever the sun looked down upon,
You must paint for me.
O, if I could only make you see
The clear blue eyes, the tender smile,
The sovereign sweetness, the gentle grace,
The woman's soul and the angel's face
That are beaming on me all the while,
But I need not speak these foolish words;
One word tells you all I would say,
She is my mother: and you will agree
That all the rest may be thrown away.

Alice Cary

Paradox

My son is quiet —
He loves to plant flowers.
He'll listen to records
In the playroom for hours.
  My daughter's a riot!
  She never sits still —
  She handles a football
  With daring and skill!
My son is mild
In temper and tone,
And his books are the key
To a world of his own.
  My daughter is wild
  And impressively loud —
  Already the leader
  Of the neighborhood crowd.
It didn't turn out
As I figured it would,
But I wouldn't change them.
(Not that I could!)
I'll fan my small Shakespeare's
Literary spark
And grab hasty kisses
From my young Joan of Arc!

Mary Dawson Hughes

My Mother

A loving heart, a helping hand,
A willingness to understand,
A ready smile, a word of cheer,
Everything that's kind and dear —
  That's my mother.

Alan Doan

Earth's Greatest Charms

God made the streams that gurgle down
   the purple mountainside;
He made the gorgeous coloring with which the sunset's dyed.
He made the hills and covered them with glory, and He made
The sparkle on the dewdrops and the flecks
   of light and shade.
Then, knowing all earth needed was a climax for her charms,
He made a little woman with a baby in her arms.

He made the arching rainbow that is thrown across the sky.
He made the blessed flowers that nod and smile as we go by.
He made the gladsome beauty as she bows with queenly grace,
But, sweetest of them all, He made the love-light
   in the face
That bends above a baby, warding off the world's alarms —
That dainty little woman with her baby in her arms.

A soft pink wrap embellished with a vine in silken thread,
A filmy snow-white cap upon a downy little head,
A dress, 'twould make the winter drift look dusty
   by its side,
Two cheeks, with pure rose petal tint,
   two blue eyes wonder-wide,
And, bending o'er, the mother face embued
   with heaven's own charms —
God bless the little woman with her baby in her arms!

Author Unknown

*B*lessed be the hand that prepares
    a pleasure for a child,
   for there is no saying when
    and where it may bloom forth.

Douglas Jerrold

A Mother's Prayer

I know so well the beauty of neat rooms —
White curtains and the warmth of polished brass,
Wide windowsills with plants in colored rows,
Serenity that shines in polished glass.
But these, dear God, are not important things,
Nor will they leave their mark in days to be.
My children may forget my ordered rooms,
In after years, but when they think of me,
May they remember I laughed much, dear God,
And heard their dreams and shared their gaiety.
And that I read them stories from old books
Of brave, fair days, and sometimes made them see
A wider world — beyond our sturdy walls.
Make them remember that I deemed it more
My task to be as gentle as I could
Than keep clean rugs upon a dusted floor.

Helen Welshimer

Home

Home is the sound of happy voices;
Home is cookies in the oven,
A little bit of scoldin'
And a great big heap of lovin' —
Home is a cheery fire,
A door that's always open —
Someone to share your secret dreams
And hope the things you're hopin';
Home is windows always lighted
And the warmth of love inside,
A little bit of heaven
Where peace and joy reside!

Rita Davis

Mother Dear

Dear Mother, you are part of me...And I am part of you...
And you are part of everything...I ever think or do...
And out of all the parts of life...I am or hope to be...
I need not tell you, Mother dear...You are the best in
me...You are the sweetest of my songs...The truest of
my friends...You are the sunshine in my heart...The
dream that never ends...You are the hand that comforts
me...The smile that lifts me up...And you are all the
sugar at...The bottom of my cup...Oh, Mother dear, there
are some things...I cannot write or say...But all my
love and gratitude...Go out to you today!

James J. Metcalfe

Mothers

The world is a marvelous
　　Spinning top
Of great affairs
　　That never stop.
Broad as the nations,
　　It narrows down
To the little streets
　　Of a friendly town;
Uncles and aunts
　　And sisters and brothers,
To the tempered point
　　That it spins on —
　　　　Mothers!

Anne Trumbull

The Family

The family
  is like a garden,
  with joy
  for all to share,
With tender, growing blossoms
  that thrive on love
  and care,
And when
  the flowers are gathered
For a very special day,
They make
  a bright and beautiful
  happiness bouquet.

Mary Alice Loberg

Love is found
  in a quiet place,
  in soft, sweet words...
  in a mother's face.

Karen Middaugh

Mother is the heart of a home.

Steven Rustad

When Mother Sleeps

When mother sleeps, a slamming door
   Disturbs her not at all;
A man might walk across the floor
   Or wander through the hall;
A pistol shot outside would not
   Drive slumber from her eyes —
But she is always on the spot
   The moment baby cries.

The thunder crash she would not hear,
   Not shouting in the street;
A barking dog, however near,
   Of sleep can never cheat
Dear Mother, but I've noticed this
   To my profound surprise:
That always wide-awake she is
   The moment baby cries.

However weary she may be,
   Though wrapped in slumber deep,
Somehow it always seems to me
   Her vigil she will keep.
Sound sleeper that she is, I take
   It in her heart there lies
A love that causes her to wake
   The moment baby cries.

Edgar A. Guest

A home is built
   on dreams of the future,
     memories of the past,
   and the ever-present strength
    of a mother's love.

Gale Baker Stanton

A Mother's Challenge

Every mother has the breathtaking privilege of sharing
with God in the creation of new life. She helps bring
into existence a soul that will endure for all eternity.

Every mother also has the unique honor of nurturing
and developing the bit of divine greatness in her child.
Through her loving and devoted care, this youthful
power can be directed from its earliest years to work
for the glory of God and the benefit of others and thus
contribute to its own temporal and eternal advantage.

Yes, a good mother can reach beyond the sanctuary of
her home and help renew the face of the earth.

James Keller

Memories and Mother

When Mother came to our room
To tuck us in at night,
Her face would look so gentle
In the soft, bedside light.

And though we may not always
Have behaved our best that day,
She'd let us know she loved us
In a very special way:
An extra fold to the coverlet,
A little pat, a hug,
And we'd settle down to dreamland,
Feeling safe and snug.

And of all the childhood memories
That there have ever been,
We love best to recall the times
When Mother tucked us in.

Mary Rita Hurley

An Old-Fashioned Mother

Blessed is the memory of an old-fashioned mother. It floats to us now like the beautiful perfume of some woodland blossoms. The music of our voices may be lost, but the entrancing melody of hers will echo in our soul forever. Other faces will fade away and be forgotten, but hers will shine on until the light from heaven's portal will glorify our own.

Author Unknown

A Mother

When God looked down upon the earth
And chose to put new blessings there,
  Gifts from above
  To show His love,
And lighten earthly joy and care,
He gave the sky the sunset glow;
Gave fragrance to the lily's blow;
  Gave laughter gay
  To children's play,
And then to every yearning soul
He gave that gift of tenderest worth —
A Mother.

The lily's sweetness is forgotten,
And sunset splendors fade to gray;
  But fresh and dear,
  Through changing year,
Through quiet night, or eager day,
The love of her we love the best
Lives closely shrined within each breast.
  Bless Heaven for —
  A Mother.

Sarah N. Latham

28

What Mother is to Me

A song of hope, a fervent prayer;
A noble dream, and tender care;
A light of truth that makes me free —
All this my mother is to me.

A bank to put my worries in;
A balm to soothe my woes and sin;
A comforter where'er I be —
All this my mother is to me.

An eager heart my joys to share;
A valiant soul to bid me dare
The shining heights her eyes can see —
All this my mother is to me.

The one who loves with all her heart;
The one who always does her part
To help and guide so patiently —
All this my mother is to me.

An artist, poet, saint, or seer;
A fragrant flower, a memory dear —
My thoughts and words fail utterly
To tell what mother is to me.

J. Harold Gwynne

Strength and dignity are her clothing,
        and she laughs at the time to come.
She opens her mouth with wisdom,
        and the teaching of kindness is on her tongue.
She looks well to the ways of her household,
        and does not eat the bread of idleness.
Her children rise up and call her blessed....

Proverbs 31:25-28

Dearest Mother

There's something about a mother
That makes her mean so much —
There's a gentle softness in her voice,
A magic in her touch —
There's something about a mother
That makes her seem so wise —
A special comfort in her smile
And loveshine in her eyes.
There's something about a mother
That makes her somehow know
How to take a hurt away
And how to make love grow.
There's something about a mother
That makes her hear each call —
And there's something about my mother
That makes her the dearest of all.

Karen Ravn

Whatever is good and true in my thoughts,
    Whatever is beautiful and joyful in my spirit,
Whatever is courageous in my actions,
    Whatever is faithful and understanding in my heart —
Are gifts from my wonderful mother.

Barbara Kunz Loots

The most beautiful word in our language is *mother*. Her
tender hands wrought for us before we entered the world.
Her weary feet never failed to carry her at night to see
that we were safe in dreamland. In the long, dark hours
she watched and prayed. She shared our sorrows and gave
us our joys.

Author Unknown

God Created Love

God created everything:
The golden daffodils,
The serenade of birds that sing,
The green and rolling hills.
He made the rainbow in the sky,
The meadows and the lanes.
He made each lovely butterfly,
The mountains and the plains.
He made the summer breeze so mild,
The moon and stars above,
But when He created Mother —
Then God created love.

Raymond Mathews

Mother and *Love*
    differ only in name,
For the miracles they work
        are one and the same.

Karl Lawrence

For when you looked into my mother's eyes you knew,
    as if He had told you, why God sent her
        into the world — it was to open the minds
        of all who looked, to beautiful thoughts.

James M. Barrie

When Amy Helps Me Cook

We use every burner on the stove
And every bowl and pan I own —
We let imaginations roam
When Amy helps me cook.
When we make cookies or cake or pie,
We always exhaust the flour supply —
We wear the most part, she and I,
When Amy helps me cook.
Of course, it takes me twice as long,
And things have a way of going wrong,
But my kitchen's filled with happy song
When Amy helps me cook.
Her daddy is free with the compliments;
He'll even eat our "accidents,"
For Love is the main ingredient
When Amy helps me cook.

Margaret Lindsey

The word *mother* has never been completely defined,
for the earth is not acquainted
with such divine words.

Charles Morgan

Happiness makes its home
in hearts furnished with love.

Hadin Marshall

I'd Rather

I'd rather be a mother
Than anyone on earth —
Bring up a child or two
Of unpretentious birth.

I'd rather tuck a little child
All safe and sound in bed —
Than twine a chain of diamonds
About my foolish head.

I'd rather wash a smudgy face
With round, bright baby eyes —
Than paint the pageantry of fame,
Or walk among the wise.

Meredith Gray

Mother is the name for God in the lips and hearts
of little children.

William Makepeace Thackeray

Planting Time

She has so much to do — there are never enough hours
in the day for everything — yet she insists on planting
her garden. With a smile she says, "I love watching
beautiful things grow." She knows that she is planting
more than just roses, pansies, cornflowers and marigolds.
Much more! She is really planting two gardens. The
rich earth will nurture flowers that will lend their
beauty for a time, but her "little helper" is the planting
ground for other seeds — of kindness, gentleness,
responsibility and idealism — and she loves to help
beautiful things grow.

Gail Cunningham

A mother has, perhaps, the hardest earthly lot.
Yet no mother worthy of the name ever
gave herself thoroughly for her child who did not feel that,
after all, she reaped what she had sown.
Henry Ward Beecher

Half-Past Three

My friend has a yacht, a house by the sea,
But I have a boy who is half-past three.

I have no jewels, no satin gown,
But I have a boy who is butter-nut brown.

My friend has an orchid, my friend has a rose,
But I have a boy with a freckled nose.

O gull, tell the waves that I have no yacht.
Wind, tell the wild forget-me-not

That I have no jewels, no shimmering gown,
No satin slippers, no pillows of down,

But I have a robin, a wind-swept hill,
A pocket of dreams, a heart to fill,

And I have a boy who is half-past three —
A little lad who looks like me.

Emily Carey Alleman

A mother always knows what you need...
sometimes that's all you need to know.

Karen Ravn

Everyday Madonna

When Father carved our Christmas bird
And asked us each what we preferred,
As sure as summer follows spring
Came Mother's, "Please, I'll take a wing."

We children never wondered why
She did not sometimes take a thigh
Or choose a drumstick or a breast.
We thought she liked a wing the best.

She said it with such easy voice,
It seemed so certainly her choice....
I was a man before I knew
Why mothers do the things they do.

Richard Armour

The family is one of nature's masterpieces.

George Santayana

The Magic of Mothers

There's magic in a mother's touch
And sunshine in her smile.
There's love in everything she does
To make our lives worthwhile.
We can find both hope and courage
Just by looking in her eyes;
Her laughter is a source of joy,
Her words are warm and wise.
There is kindness and compassion
To be found in her embrace,
And we see the light of heaven
Shining from a mother's face.

Reginald Holmes

Mothers have a way of making the difficult times easier
and the good times truly wonderful.

James Langdon

Flowers for Mother

I never have a special day
To give flowers to my mother;
I give them to her every day
To show how much I love her.

When I sweep the kitchen floor,
Or care for baby brother,
Run on errands, or make the beds,
I'm giving flowers to mother.

It's lots of fun pretending
And to hear my mother say,
"Thank you, dear, for all the flowers
You've given me today."

Clara Rader

Inventory of Mothers

Mothers have full cookie jars
For little girls to share,
Kisses for skinned noses, and
Her old high heels to wear.
Time to take you on her lap
To read a storybook,
Pretty aprons tied in bows
And applesauce to cook.
Scraps of cloth and bits of lace
To dress a dolly right,
Hands to tuck you safely in
At bedtime every night.

Doris Chalma Brock

The Way of a Mother

Somehow she never seems to see
The change that the years have made in me,
Her hands have the soft and gentle touch
That I, as a small child, loved so much.

Her voice, in the same familiar way,
Soothes the hurts of a too-harsh day,
And her patient love and tender care
Follow my footsteps like a prayer.

Thank God that mothers are so blind
To the babyhood we leave behind,
For often in life, with its care and pain,
It is sweet to be thought a child again.

Katherine Edelman

Nothing speaks so loudly, or is heard so plainly,
as the silent voice of a mother's love.

Emily Ashley Tipton

The Beauty of a Mother's Love

Like flowers in the window
make a very lovely sight,
Like sunshine after rain clouds
makes the world so warm and bright,
Like lilting flights
of butterflies
bring pleasure and delight…
There's beauty
in a mother's
special love.

Like melodies of songbirds
fill the springtime skies of blue,
Like each dawn is reflected
in the fields of sparkling dew,
Like soft and gentle breezes
make the world seem fresh and new…
There's beauty in a mother's special love.

Mary Dawson Hughes

All the love we come to know in life
springs from the love we knew as children.

James Langdon